Amy,
When you don't
know how to pray

PRAY

LIKE A

CHILD

Pray like a child !

Dan

DAN RING

9/21/2020

Blue Mountain Publishing
1100 McNatt Drive #1
Brookland, AR 72417

ISBN: 9781099237706

PREFACE

This book is for you if you have ever prayed and wondered if you got it right. It's for the educated, wise, and learned who think they know how to pray. It's for everyone who finds themselves in a place they never expected to be. It's for those who have struggled with prayer. It is for the ones who have been calloused by life's experiences. It's for you, even if you have never prayed before.

There have been times in my life that I felt like one of the disciples when they asked Jesus to teach them to pray. I didn't know if I was doing it right. I wanted my prayers to matter. I wondered if there was a better way. Surely, if I could learn more about how to pray, then maybe I could pray a prayer that would move God's heart. I may never pray the perfect prayer, but surely, I could pray better prayers.

In the eleventh chapter of Matthew, Christ says:

I praise You, Father. You have hidden these things from the wise and learned and revealed them to little children.[25] Yes, Father. You did this for Your good pleasure.[26]

Come to me, all you who are weary and burdened, and I will give you rest.[28] Take My

yoke and learn from Me.[29] My yoke is easy and

My burden is light.[30]

What if prayer was easy? If I prayed with the wonder of a child, would it change the way I prayed? Life through the eyes of a three-year-old is very different than the world you and I see. It's not that complicated when you start your day with cartoons and Cocoa Puffs.

If you are looking for the definitive guide to prayer, the one book that looks at prayer from an exhaustive analytical point of view, this is not the book for you. What I've tried to do is just the opposite. I have made every effort to sift the complex and the complicated through the filter of a child. I have looked at time spent with the Father through the eyes of a three-year-old. I have tried to recapture the innocence of prayer, before we were jaded by the pain and the suffering and the prevalence of evil. How did we pray when "black was black" and "white was white," before we saw the world in *Fifty Shades of Grey*?

PRAY LIKE A CHILD

CONTENTS

PRAY LIKE A CHILD

1

IT'S NOT THAT COMPLICATED

L ove is not that complicated. Salvation is not that complicated. Grace is not that complicated. Prayer is not that complicated. Life is just not that complicated from the perspective of a three-year-old.

One day, the disciples came to Jesus and asked, "Who is the greatest in the kingdom of heaven?" He called a little child and had him stand among them. Then He said, "I tell you the truth, unless you change and become like little children, you will never enter the kingdom of heaven". Matthew 18:1–3

Another time, Jesus said, "Let the little children come to Me, and do not hinder them, for the kingdom of heaven belongs to such as these". Matthew 19:14

Something happens as we get older. We realize that things can't be that simple any longer. We begin to complicate things; we look for more complex solutions to our problems. The bigger the problem, the more complicated and complex the solution has to be. But God, in His infinite wisdom, reminds us at times that He never intended for life to be complicated. "God is not a God of confusion or disorder, but a God of peace". 1 Corinthians 14:33

Remember, God uses the weak and the foolish and despised things of the world (simple things) to bring to nothing (the complex, the complicated) the things that are mighty. 1Corinthians 1:27

Do you remember when the Lord used a stick to defeat the king of Egypt? It was just a stick, but the Lord said to Moses and Aaron, "When Pharaoh says to you, 'Perform a miracle,' Aaron should take his staff and throw it down before Pharaoh and his officials and it will become a snake." With that stick, God performed many other miracles in the sight of Pharaoh and the people of Egypt. When Pharaoh and the people of Egypt could take no more, Moses and Aaron were summoned during the middle of the night, and Pharaoh said to them, "Go! Leave Egypt, and leave my people, you and all the Israelites. Go and worship the Lord your God."

Do you remember when Jesus took a small

boy's lunch and fed thousands of hungry people? He was just a little boy with five loaves of bread and two fish, but with that little boy's lunch, Jesus fed five thousand men, not counting the women and children. After everyone had enough to eat, Jesus said to the disciples, "Gather the pieces that are left over." They gathered twelve baskets full of leftovers.

Do you remember when Samson used the jawbone of a donkey to strike down one thousand men? God gave Samson the victory over one thousand Philistines, who were the enemy of God's people. "With the jawbone of a donkey, I have made donkeys of them," said Samson. Then Samson led Israel for twenty years in the days of the Philistines.

Do you remember the time when God used a rock to defeat the Philistines? David, the youngest son of Jesse, was the keeper of his father's sheep. He had nothing but five stones and a sling. With one of those stones and the sling, God gave David the victory over Goliath, the mighty Philistine champion. Without a sword in his hand, David struck down the Philistine and killed him. When the Philistine army saw that their hero was dead, they turned and ran.

Don't despise what seems weak and insignificant to the world. A little thing, in the hands of a big God, can bring down the things that are mighty in the world. The jawbone of a donkey, a stick, and a stone seem like a strange way to win the battle. A little boy's lunch may seem like a strange way to feed the hungry. If God can use these insignificant things to accomplish much, imagine what God can do with the prayer of a three-year-old.

God can use the prayer of a child to bring down the giants in your life!

It happened one day that while Jesus was praying in a certain place. After He had finished, one of His disciples said to Him, "Lord, teach us to pray just as John also taught his disciples". Luke 11:1

He said to them, "When you pray, first consider your need, and pray to God accordingly. If you need healing, you must pray to Jehovah-Rophe, the Lord who heals. If you troubled, you must pray to Jehovah-Shalom, the Lord our peace. If you have a specific need, you must pray to Jehovah-Jireh, the Lord who provides. If you feel lonely and helpless, you should pray to Jehovah-Shammah, the Lord who is there. If you are being attacked, you must pray to Jehovah-Sabaoth, the Lord of Hosts and the commander of angel armies. If feel weak, you need to pray to Abhir, the Mighty One. If you feel abandoned, you must pray to El Roi, the God who sees."

No! That's not what He said!

He said to them, "When you pray, say: Father, hallowed be Your name. Your kingdom come. Give us each day our daily bread. And forgive us our sins, for we ourselves also forgive everyone who is indebted to us. And lead us not into temptation" Luke 11:2-4

He said, "Say Father."

Sixty-five times in the gospels of Matthew, Mark, and Luke and over one hundred times in the gospel of John alone, Christ referred to God as Father. It was by far His favorite term for addressing God. It wasn't one of the ways He taught the disciples to pray to God. It was the way He taught them to pray to God.

When you pray, do you pray like a child talking to your Father, or do you pray to someone else?

Don't confuse what God does with who God is. The attributes of God are infinite. He is the Alpha and the Omega, the First and the Last, the Beginning and the End.

He is the Bread of Life. He is the chief Cornerstone. He is compassionate. He is the Creator. He is our defender. He is everlasting, our Emmaus love. He is our fortress and the fount of every blessing. He is the Good Shepherd and the giver of all good gifts. He is our healer, our hope, and our High Priest. He is immoveable, indescribable, invincible, and Immanuel. He is Jehovah. He is the King of kings, and the Lord of lords, and the giver of life and the keeper of my soul. He is the Lion and the Lamb. He is merciful. There is none like Him. There is none beside Him, and there is none before Him. He is omnipotent, omnipresent, and omniscient. He is the One and Only, the Only One, and the only wise God. He is the Prince of Peace. He is all-powerful. He is perfect. He is quintessential. He is my Rock and my Refuge. He is my Redeemer, my Rebuilder, and my Restorer. He is my Strong Tower, my Strength, and my Safe Harbor. He is the three in one God, and He is the only God. He is undeniable, unsearchable, undefeatable, and unparalleled. He is the Victorious Warrior. He is wise, worthy, and without fault. He is a wonderful, Counselor. He is Yahweh.

Before my dad died, he was many things to me. He was my disciplinarian. He was my friend. He was my little league coach. He was a mechanic. He was a welder. He was a pipe fitter. He was a salesman. He drove a milk truck. He taught me how to hunt and fish. He taught me how to ride a bike and drive a car. He taught me how a man should treat a woman. He showed me who God was and taught me how to live. He did many more things before he died, but what my dad did is not who my dad was. He was my father.

Jesus said, "When you pray, say 'Father.'"

The Bible gives many names by which we can call upon our God. He is Elohim, God our Creator. He is El Shaddai, God Almighty. He is Adonai, the Lord is my master. He is Jehovah, Lord. He is Jehovah-Jireh, the Lord our provider. He is Jehovah-Rophe, the Lord who heals. He is Jehovah-Nissi, the Lord our banner. He is Jehovah-M'kaddesh, the Lord who sanctifies. He is

Jehovah-Shalom, the Lord our peace. He is Jehovah Elohim, Lord God. He is Jehovah-Tsidkenu, the Lord our righteousness. He is Jehovah-Rohi, the Lord our shepherd. He is Jehovah-Shammah, the Lord is there. He is Jehovah-Sabaoth, the Lord of hosts and the commander of angel armies. He is El Elyon, the Most High God. He is Abhir, the Mighty One. He is Kadosh, the Holy One. He is El Roi, the God of seeing.

These are just some of the many names given by which we can call out to God, but I believe His favorite name is "Father."

Jesus said to them, "When you pray, Say Father."

Pray like a child talking to your Father.

2

PRAY UNTIL IT RAINS

S atan says, "How many times will you ask God for the same thing over and over? If God wanted to answer your prayer, He could have done it by now. How many more times will you ask God before He looks at you and says, "My child, if you just had a little faith, don't you know that I heard you the first time you asked? Don't you know that I knew what you needed before you even asked?"

In the fourteenth chapter of the gospel of Mark, Christ prayed at Gethsemane. He said to His disciples, "Sit here while I pray."[32] Going a little farther, He fell to the ground and prayed that if it were possible, the hour might pass from Him.[35] Then He returned to the disciples and found them sleeping.[37] Once more, He went away and prayed the same thing.[39]

Once more, the Beloved Son prayed to His Heavenly Father, and He prayed the same thing again.

Is it a lack of faith if we continually ask for the same thing over and over again? Or is it an act of faith, knowing that God hears every cry of our heart? I am convinced that it is an act of faith, when we believe that God is a good Father who is able to do exceedingly and abundantly more than we can ask or even imagine.

God will never grow tired of hearing His children pray. In the eighteenth chapter of Luke, Jesus tells the disciples a parable to show them that they should always pray and not give up. He says, "Will God [your Father who has chosen you] not answer you when you cry out to Him day and night [continually]?[7] But will the Son of Man find such persistent faith on the earth when He comes?"[8]

When we think about faith, do we think about the quality of our faith, or do we think about the quantity of our faith? Great faith, or little faith, or faith the size of a mustard seed, these are measures of the quantity of our faith. Jesus never put an emphasis on the quantity of our faith. To the contrary, He said, "If you have faith the size of a mustard seed [a little faith], you can say to this mountain, 'Move from here to there' and it will move. Nothing will be impossible for you". Matthew 17:20

Persistent faith is not a little faith; nor is it great faith. Persistent faith is a faith that perseveres in spite of opposition, obstacles, and discouragement. It continues in the face of persecution. It is an enduring faith that remains when the healing does not come. Persistent faith never gives up, never gives in, and never quits.

Do you pray with the persistent faith of a child?

I was at Walmart recently. As I started down the aisle with the cookies, I noticed a young mother and her small child. He looked to be three to four years old. He was a handsome little man with blond hair and big blue eyes. As the mother attempted to move right past the cookies without slowing down, her little boy reached for the cookies and said, "Cookies please. Cookies."

The young mother smiled at her little boy and said, "No. We're not getting cookies."

He smiled right back and said, "Cookies please. Pretty please."

She got in his face and giggled as they rubbed noses and said, "No cookies."

He said, "Please. Pretty please. Please."

I felt bad as I got my cookies. I really hoped the

little guy didn't see me. I tried to hide them underneath my bread. As we turned the corner and started down the cereal aisle, the little boy seemed to forget about the cookies. Something else had caught his eye; it was Sonny the Cuckoo Bird on the Cocoa Puffs cereal box. He reached for the Cocoa Puffs, looked at his mother, and smiled as he said, "Cocoa Puffs please."

She smiled right back at him and said, "No. No Cocoa Puffs."

He smiled, looked at her with those big blue eyes, and said, "Please, Mommy. Pretty please. Cocoa Puffs."

As she put a box of Cheerios in the cart, she smiled and said, "No Cocoa Puffs."

Once more he said, "Please, Mommy. Pretty please."

She laughed as she tickled him and said, "No Cocoa Puffs."

Not quite ready to give up, he smiled at his mother and said, "Cookies. Pretty please."

I laughed out loud. She turned and smiled at me. It was obvious that she loved her little man and this was a game they had played several times before. I honestly think she enjoyed hearing her child say please.

How much more does our Heavenly Father

delight to hear His children cry out day and night, saying, "Please, Daddy, pretty please"?

The next aisle over were the soft drinks.

"Dr. Pepper, Mommy. Please. Pretty please."

"No. No Dr. Pepper," she said as she tickled him.

"Cocoa Puffs, Mommy. Please."

"No. No Cocoa Puffs."

"Cookies. Pretty please."

He was persistent. He never whined. He didn't pout. He didn't throw a fit. He smiled. He said please. And he didn't give up.

I thought to myself, *When I pray, am I as persistent as a child?*

Recently, a friend asked me to pray for his wife. She had been diagnosed with a triple negative invasive ductile carcinoma breast cancer. I said that I would pray because I believe in the power of prayer. I believe the effective fervent prayer of a righteous man accomplishes much. James 5:16

James tells us to pray for one another so that we may be healed. But I also believe the two verses that follow. Verse seventeen says that Elijah was a man just like us, and he prayed earnestly that it would not rain, and it did not rain on the land for three- and one-half years. Verse eighteen says that Elijah prayed again, and the heavens opened, and it rained, and the earth produced its crops. If you go back to 1 Kings, chapter eighteen and read the full account, Elijah did not pray for rain one time or twice or even three times. He prayed until it rained. Seven times as Elijah prayed, he told his servant to go and look to see if it was raining. The seventh time, his servant said, "I see a cloud as small as a man's hand rising up from the sea." The sky grew black with clouds, the wind rose, the heavens opened, and a heavy rain came on the land.

I told my friend, "We will pray, and we will pray until it rains!"

You can pray without ceasing. You can pray with the persistence of a child, but if you are praying a dumb prayer, don't be surprised if nothing changes. James 5:16 does not say, "The dumb prayer, offered with great fervor and passion, by a righteous man accomplishes much." I don't care how passionate or how fervent your prayer may be. If it is a dumb prayer, you can persist until Jesus comes back. Your fervor and your passion and your persistence will probably be for naught. I should know. I prayed a dumb prayer, with much fervor and passion, persistently for a long time.

Debbie and I had been married for fifteen years, and up to this point, I had only done one really dumb thing. Oh, I was guilty of many minor infractions. I am a guy, and guys do dumb things. God made man from dirt, and there are times when we are as dumb as dirt. My award for being the dumbest man alive came one day as I was playing cards with a bunch of other guys. We were in the employees' lounge. It was lunchtime, and the choices consisted of the typical vending machine cuisine, honey buns, chips, candy bars, and sodas. The room was dark and gloomy and filled with smoke. The back door opened, and in walked this goddess, an angel, a radiant beauty that turned every man's head. She had beautiful big brown eyes. Her smile rivaled the rising sun. I don't think she even noticed that everyone in the room was looking at her as she walked up to me. She brought me lunch. She had fixed me a ham-and-cheese sandwich. She packed chips, a pickle, and one of those little candy bars, and she brought me a Coke. The best part of all was the smile on her face. At that moment, I was the envy of every man in that room. Not only was she beautiful, she had brought me lunch.

I took one bite of the sandwich, and I can only imagine the look on my face as I said to her in unbelief, "You put the mustard next to the cheese?" Instead of being grateful, I was critical. Instantly, the only light in that dark and smoke-filled room went out. I did not mean to, but I had cut her to the core with my hurtful words in front of every other man in that room. I may have been the youngest man in the room, but that was no excuse for being the dumbest. Without hesitation, an older man sitting at the same table as me—a much wiser man than me, a man who understood the magnitude of the *dumbness* of what I had just done—proceeded to put me in my place. He rebuked me, but it was too late. The smile that had brightened the entire room had disappeared, and those big brown eyes were beginning to swell up with puppy-dog tears. The beautiful young girl that had walked into the room with a smile on her face looked like a little whipped puppy as she walked out. I was young, but how could I have been so *dumb*?

I learned my lesson that day. I never made that mistake again. There were other lessons to be learned, and for the next fifteen years, I continued to learn how not to be so dumb. I was doing good, no major infractions, until we moved back to Northeast Arkansas. I was older, and I should have been wiser, but I wasn't. We had three children and no money. I was struggling to build an insurance practice, and I was about to make the biggest mistake of my life.

To help pay the bills, my wife, Debbie, decided to work outside the home in a factory until we could get caught up. The plan was for her to work there only until we got caught up; then she would help me grow the insurance business.

Debbie would get up at four o'clock in the morning to be at work on time. She was out of place in that factory. She was as much out of place as she was the day she walked into that dark and smoke-filled employee lounge, but she never complained. I would get up as she was leaving for work and get the kids up, feed them breakfast, and get them to school on time. Debbie was home from work by the time the kids got home from school. I helped with supper and the dishes. Most times, we had the kids in bed between eight o'clock and eight thirty in the evening. By nine o'clock, Debbie was ready for bed. There never seemed to be any time for just the two of us. If I did go to bed with her, she was always tired. We didn't talk much, and we continued to struggle financially. To make a long story short, there was no money, no conversation, and no intimacy. Any one of those three things can put a strain on a relationship, but all three at the same time is a recipe for disaster. I felt rejected. This was not the girl that I had fallen in love with. I will say it again: there was no money, no conversation and no intimacy. It was not a pretty picture, and I was not a happy man.

I began to pray persistently with great fervor and passion. I prayed, "Oh God, change this woman. Please!" Continually, I prayed. It didn't seem to matter how passionate or how fervent and how persistent I was. Nothing changed.

I did not realize it at the time, but I was praying a dumb prayer. I believed that she was wrong and that she was mistreating me, and I wasn't happy. Then one day, I read that familiar passage in Ephesians.

"Husbands, love your wife as Christ loved the church."
Wow! I thought, If Christ loved me in spite of my
shortcomings and failures and my sometimes-blatant
sin, then maybe I should try to love her even if she was
wrong and still mistreating me.

I resolved to pray a different prayer. I began to
pray that God would help me to love her as He loved
me. I prayed that He would help me to see her as He
saw her, even though she was wrong. This wasn't the
best prayer, but it was better than the dumb prayer I
had been praying. I still believed that I was right, that
she was wrong, and that she was mistreating me. But I
wanted to love her like Christ loved her, like He loved
me. With fervor and passion, I prayed the God would
change me. I did not pray that God would change her. I
prayed that He would change me. And it didn't take
long for God to answer that prayer.

How could I have been so dumb again?

She didn't love me any less. She was not looking
for conversation and intimacy somewhere else. She was
just tired. She was getting up at four o'clock every
morning or sometimes earlier, and I wasn't. I was
wrong. I was dumb, even though I was older now. I had
been praying a dumb prayer with persistence, passion,
and fervor. I had been asking God for Cocoa Puffs, Dr.
Pepper, and cookies with the persistence of a small
child. Over and over again, I said, "Please, God. Pretty
please." I was expecting God to change her. I was

diligently asking God to change her.

Was God disappointed with my persistence and passion, as misguided as it was? No! He just smiled because He knew I didn't need what I had been asking for. He knew I was the one who needed to change. And when I got that right, He was happy. He was eager to give me what I asked for.

Pray with the persistence of a child.

Pray until it rains, but don't pray dumb prayers.

3

I HAVE LEARNED THAT MY GOD HEARS ME WHEN I PRAY

How can a God who has created all things and by whom all things that have been created are held together be attentive and give an ear to my petitions? Why would a God who orders the wind and the waves be concerned with my problems? Why would a God who seeks council from no man listen to me? With a world in chaos, as nations rise against nations, and the hearts of men have been turned toward everything except God, does God even hear me when I pray? If God does hear the cries of His children, does He really care about my needs when there are so many others with greater needs than me? I am just a voice in the crowd crying out for mercy and grace. Like the paralytic at the pool of Bethesda, there were times that I wished I had a friend to carry me, someone to pray with me, and to make a noise loud enough with me that Jesus would hear our cries of desperation.

I grew up in the church. I accepted Christ as my Lord and Savior at a very early age. I don't ever remember a time when I didn't pray. We always prayed before meals, and every night before I went to bed, I said my prayers. But there are times in the life of every believer when our circumstance changes the way we pray, and prayer becomes more than just something we do before we eat or go to sleep.

It wasn't until my dad was diagnosed with leukemia that my prayer life moved to a whole other level. This wasn't a fever or a sore throat. This was cancer, and this was serious. There had been times before when prayer was important. I remember when Jennifer, our little girl, was six months old, we thought we had lost her. Debbie called me at work. Jennifer's temperature was one hundred five degrees and rising. I got there before the ambulance did. As I held my little girl, she went into a seizure, and then her eyes rolled back into her head, and her little body went limp. I held her lifeless body up over my head and cried out in desperation, "Oh God, don't take our little girl. Don't take our baby."

With two brothers, there were more bumps and

bruises and fevers and sore throats and stitches and accidents that kept us on our knees. Having children will teach you how to pray. But this was different. This was cancer, and this was my dad. This changed everything. For three years, we prayed for healing, believing in miracles, and then on October 20, 1998, my dad died.

On August 28, 2001, Debbie was diagnosed with stage-4 colon cancer. She was forty-four years old. Jason, our oldest son, was twenty-one; Jennifer was twenty, and Adam was just sixteen. Four days later, she had surgery to remove the tumor. Five days after the surgery, we went home so that she could rest before chemotherapy treatments began. It was Tuesday, September 11, and getting back to the office to take care of my clients was not very high on my list of priorities. Taking care of my wife was more important. At this point, I didn't know when I would go back to work. Trying to hold on to some sense of normalcy, I started the day as I had most every other day. I went out for an early morning run. I had no intentions of going to the office that day, so I didn't get started as early as usual. After an easy run, and time to spend a few minutes alone reflecting on the disorder and chaos of the past couple of weeks, I made it back home. As I walked in the back door, Debbie was resting on the couch, and she was calling for me to come quickly. I hurried to her side. Together, we watched in silence and disbelief the breaking news as the events that morning unfolded on national television. The north tower of the

World Trade Center in New York City had been struck by an American Airlines Boeing 767. The impact left a gaping, burning hole near the eightieth floor of the one-hundred-ten-story skyscraper, instantly killing hundreds of people and trapping hundreds more on higher floors. As the evacuation of both towers got underway, television cameras broadcasted live images of what initially appeared to be a freak accident. Then eighteen minutes after the first plane hit, a second Boeing 767—this time of United Airlines—appeared out of the sky, turned sharply toward the World Trade Center, and sliced into the south tower near the sixtieth floor. The collision caused a massive explosion that showered burning debris over surrounding buildings and the streets below. This nation was under attack, and we never saw it coming. As we watched in disbelief, I could not help but feel compassion for the victims as these tragic events were taking place. Somehow, at the same time, it all seemed so distant. We had our own tragedy, right there in our living room, overwhelming our lives. We never saw it coming.

In the quietness of that moment, I began to pray. I did not pray for the victims or their families or the first responders. I prayed for my wife. Our world had been turned upside down. The desperation in our lives, in our living room at that moment, was more real than what we were watching on television.

Cancer had taken my dad, and I did not want cancer to win again. As I prayed, the Spirit of God revealed to me this truth: my prayer is never diluted by the prayers of others. This was a time when our nation cried out to God in unison with a loud and mighty voice. I doubt that there has ever been a moment in time, during my lifetime, when the collective prayers of this nation were so numerous. Even so, my humble prayer broke through the collective prayers of this nation. It was not that my prayer was any more significant or any more important to God. It wasn't. But here is the good news, my prayer was no less significant and no less important to God than any other prayer at that moment in time.

I had an audience of one with the King of kings and Lord of lords.

There was never a time when I doubted that God heard me when I prayed that day. I knew He heard my prayer, but two years later, God confirmed through His word the very truth He had spoken through His Spirit to me on that day.

I was reading in the tenth chapter of Mark, verses 46–52. It's the story of the healing of blind Bartimaeus. Jesus, His disciples, and a great multitude went out of Jericho on their way to Jerusalem. Blind Bartimaeus sat by the road, begging. He must have been far enough removed from the road that many did not even take notice of him. There is no account of the disciples even acknowledging this desperate beggar as he cried, "Jesus, Son of David, have mercy on me."

Were the disciples indifferent or were they just preoccupied with what was happening in the moment? Did they not have compassion, or was the cry of a beggar drowned out by noise and the crowd and the prevailing chaos? There were some who heard the cry of this desperate beggar. Some did take notice. We are told they warned him to be quiet, but he cried all the more. Then in the midst of the multitude, chaos, and noise, Jesus stopped. He stood still, and it was as if time stood still. Those who had rebuked Bartimaeus were silenced. The one who had been despised by others was exalted to the place of honor. The outcast was welcomed in. The one who had been rejected by the social elites was accepted at the King's table. The beggar was given an audience of one, in the midst of the multitude, noise, and chaos, with the King of kings and the Lord of lords.

Your prayers are never diluted by the prayers of others. When the noise, chaos, and confusion of this world seems overwhelming and the prayers of others are staggering, He stills hears the beggar's cry.

Pray like a small child, believing that God hears you when you pray. Pray like a beggar crying out for mercy.

A child is never concerned that someone else may have something to say that is more important than what they have to say. Don't worry that someone else may be praying at the same time you are. Don't ever be concerned that the prayers of others might carry more weight or importance than your prayer. Don't ever think that maybe somehow your prayers could get lost in the noise, confusion, and chaos of this world.

Pray like a child, believing that your Father hears every prayer and sees every tear. Pray knowing that you are loved by the Father and that there is no power or principality, no angel above or demon below, nothing present or anything to come, nothing in life or death, and nothing is too high, and nothing is too deep enough. There is no created thing that will ever be able to separate you from the love of God your Father that is secure in Christ Jesus the Lord.

Pray like you are an only child, and you have an audience of one with your Father.

4

HOW FOCUSED ARE YOUR PRAYERS

H ave you ever noticed that a child's prayer seems to be more focused and to the point? Children are very specific when they pray. But something happens as we get older. The distractions of this world, the chaotic life we live, and the pressures of family and our jobs may cause us to lose our focus when we pray. Our prayers become more scattered. Like Martha, we can easily be drawn away from the one thing that is important, and we begin to worry and get upset over many other things. We use more words and bigger words as we pray, and we pray about more things. But what are we really saying? Do our prayers reflect how busy we are, or do our prayers reflect how

26

focused we are?

If a child listened to you pray, would they know what was important to you?

When they pray, a child's prayer may seem scattered, even unorganized as they give thanks. They seem to be grateful for the things we take for granted as we get older. "Thank you, Jesus, for our homes and the builders who build them so we will have a place to live. Thank you for the bricks and windows and doors they use to build our homes. Thank you for our food and the farmers who grow our food. Thank you for the ice cream and cake. Thank you for the money so we can buy food. Thank you for cars and bikes and video games and family and moms and dads and grandmas and grandpas."

When a child gives thanks, they are grateful for many things, but when a child petitions Christ, it's usually laser focused. "Help Mommy get a job. Help Mommy's head stop hurting. Make sissy's belly feel better. Touch Daddy's back and take away the pain. Watch over us, Jesus. Keep us safe."

When I pray, do I pray intentional, focused prayers? Or do I use a lot of words? Do I use bigger words and pray about many things? Do my prayers reflect what is really important, or do they reflect how busy I am?

Who told us that by simply bringing something

to God's attention, we have prayed an effective prayer, as if God needs to be informed about all that is going on? Why do we think that we have made a difference when all we have done is tell God what He already knows?

We pray for God to feed the hungry. There are people in other parts of the world who have very little to eat. If You don't feed them, they will die. I know You love them Lord. Please take care of them. There are people in America who go to bed hungry, Lord. Please! Please, Lord, let them know that You love them. Lord, there are people who couldn't make it if it weren't for mission outreach and the local food bank. Please don't let anybody go hungry. There are children who go to the same school as my children who only eat what they get at school each day. Lord, please love these kids. Oh, if I just had enough faith, then surely, I could pray a James 5:16 prayer for the hungry, and it would make a difference. Lord, please give me the kind of faith to pray that kind of prayer.

We pray, "Lord there are so many homeless. Some of them just need a little help, Lord. Some of the homeless are the ones who go to bed hungry. They can't provide for themselves or their families. They don't have jobs, Lord. Please help them, Lord. Some of them are our veterans who have given so much for this country, and now the government is falling short in providing for their basic needs. It's not right, Lord. I know You love them. Please wrap Your arms around them and comfort them."

"Lord, there are so many who have cancer today."

"Lord, there are so many who are dealing with drugs and alcohol today."

"Lord, there are so many children who are being abused today."

"Lord, there are so many single moms today, struggling to provide for their children."

"Lord, our schools are a mess today."

"Lord, our government is a mess today."

We pray for God to move and do what only He can do; but seldom do we pray for God to move through us. There is a price to be paid if we will be used by God. We will pay the price to pray a prayer, then count the cost if He says, "Go here or there." We will pay the price to pray for God to right the wrongs, to heal our land, to feed the hungry, to visit the lonely, and to rescue the children. But how eager are we to be used by God to meet these needs?

We cry out, "Lord, please give me the kind of faith to pray a prayer that moves Your heart." We want to pray a prayer that avails much, a prayer that moves mountains, a prayer that changes things, a prayer that makes a difference. We want the kind of faith it takes to pray that kind of prayer. We will pay the price to pray the prayer.

Then God says, "It is not about how much faith you have." Jesus taught the disciples that all it takes is a little faith. He said that with a measure of faith as small as a mustard seed, they could speak to the mountains, and the mountains would obey. The object of your faith is more important than the size of your faith. I'll say that again. The object of your faith, the size of your God, is more important than the size of your faith. Faith without compassion is of little use. What good is it to have great faith if you have no compassion for others? If I see someone in need, if I see someone who is hungry, if I see someone who needs clothes, or if I see someone who needs a place to stay and I do nothing, what good is my faith? If I say to the one in need, "Go your way. I wish you well. I will pray for you. I will pray that God will supply your needs because I have great faith." But if I do nothing about his physical needs, what good is my faith?

Faith is good, but faith without deeds is dead. Faith without love is nothing. God said that you can have all faith, so much faith that you can move mountains, but if you don't have love, you are nothing. He didn't say if you have *some* faith. He didn't say if you have *a little* faith. He didn't say if you have *great* faith. He said that you can have *all* faith. But if you don't have love, you have nothing. 1 Corinthians 13:2

Jesus said, "This is how the world will know that you are My disciples, if you have love for one another". John 13:35

I wanted to pray with great faith, mountain-moving faith. I wanted my prayers to make a difference.

He wanted me to pray with great love.

The key to praying an effective fervent prayer that accomplishes much is not to be found in how fervent our prayer is. Persistence is important. Praying with passion is important. A flippant prayer is not a fervent prayer. Jesus told His disciples a parable to show them that they should always pray and never give up. Luke 18:1

Never quit! Never stop! Never give up! There should be a fire in our soul when we pray that burns without ceasing.

The key to praying an effective prayer that accomplishes much is not to be found in our righteousness either. Apart from the righteousness of Christ, we have no righteousness. A righteous man praying an effective fervent prayer that accomplishes much is the man or woman who comes boldly before the throne of grace covered in the righteousness of Christ. Before I come, before I ascend the hill of the Lord, before I stand in His holy place, let me examine myself. Am I covered by the righteousness of Christ? If not, then it is foolishness for me to think that I could come before a holy God with clean hands and a pure heart. Even as believers, on our best days, we still get it wrong sometimes. We ask with great fervor and passion. We are persistent. But we may be asking with selfish motives. How do I know that? He said we do. He said, "Sometimes you ask, and you do not receive because you ask with the wrong motives". James 4:3

Our fervor, our passion, our persistence, and our motives will never matter if our righteousness is self-righteousness. Our righteousness will never be enough. The only difference between the righteousness of a believer and the righteousness of a nonbeliever is the righteousness of Christ and Christ alone.

The key to praying an effective fervent prayer that accomplishes much may be found in the depth of our love. Someone once said, "That love can be spelled *time*." If I love you, then I will have time for you. If I don't have time for you, then I don't really love you. Love is a verb. Love conveys a willingness on our part to take action. The Greek word that was translated effective in James 5:16 is the word energeo. It is a verb from which we get our word energy. It means active, to be at work, to be operative, to put forth effort or power. A James 5:16 prayer that accomplishes much is an active prayer. It is not a passive prayer.

We see the same Greek word used in:

Hebrews 4:12—"The word of God is living and

active. Sharper than a double-edged sword."

Matthew 14:1–2—"At that time Herod the tetrarch heard about Jesus, and he said to his attendants, 'This is John the Baptist; he has risen from the dead, and that is why miraculous powers are *at work* in him.'"

Galatians 2:8—"For God, who was *at work* in the ministry of Peter as an apostle to the Jews, was also *at work* in my ministry as an apostle to the Gentiles."

Galatians 3:5—"Does God give you His Spirit and *work* miracles among you because you observe the law, or because you believe what you heard?"

Galatians 5:6—"For in Christ Jesus neither circumcision nor uncircumcision has any value. The only thing that counts is faith *working* through love."

Ephesians 1:11—"In Him we were also chosen, having been predestined according to the plan of Him who *works out* everything in conformity with the purpose of His will."

These are just a few of the other times we see the same word that is translated effective in James 5:16 used in the New Testament. Each time, there is activity associated with this word, not passivity.

If I truly have a passion for the hungry, the

effective prayer that accomplishes much is not the passionate prayer offered in faith asking God to feed the hungry. The effective prayer that will accomplish much is the prayer that cries out, "Oh God, here I am. Send me. Use me. I don't know what I can do, but show me what You would have me to do. Help me to love the hungry." If you pray that prayer, God may use you to make a difference in the world, or God may use you to make a difference in the life of your neighbor. Either way, that prayer will change someone's world.

Pray that God would use you to love the hurting. Pray that God would use you to love the homeless. Pray that God would use you to love the sick.

Pray passionate prays. Pray bold prayers. Pray focused prayers. Pray effective prayers. You may not be able to change the world with your prayers, but if you are willing to pray an effective prayer, an active prayer, a prayer that is motivated by love, God will change someone's world through you.

Pray like a child with a deliberate focus.

Pray for what is really important to you. Find your passion. Pray for what God has burdened your heart with. And pray that God would use you.

If you really want your prayers to be more focused, pray like you were dying. Nothing will sharpen your focus like embracing your own mortality. Most of us would rather not face the fact that God has appointed a time for each of us to die.

We say, "Today or tomorrow, we will go to this city or that city, spend time there, carry on business, and make money". James 4:13

We say, "This is what I'll do. I'll tear down my barns and build bigger ones, and there I will store all my grain and goods.[18] I'll say to myself, "You have plenty of good things laid up for many years. Take life easy; eat, drink and be merry".[19] Luke 12:18–19

We may not tear down barns to build bigger ones, unless we happen to be a farmer. But we will strive for the bigger house, the newer car, and laying up for ourselves the pleasures of this world so that we will have good things laid up for many years.

In the blink of an eye, it all changes. You go to the doctor and get a bad report. What was important is suddenly not so important anymore. You quit smoking. You quit drinking. You lose weight. You start exercising. You change your diet, all because you realize that you will die one day, and if something does not change, that day may come quickly. If embracing your own mortality changes the way you live, don't you think it would also change the way you pray?

You would probably pray with more urgency. You would probably pray more deliberately.

You would pray about what was important.

Your prayers would be more focused.

Pray focused prayers.

Pray that God would use you.

Pray like you were dying!

5

PRAY FOR GOD'S BLESSING

How do you pray when you don't know what to pray? How do you know if your praying the Father's will? We all know the promise of 1 John 5:14–15. "This is the assurance we have in approaching God: that if we ask anything according to His will, He hears us.[14] And if we know that He hears us—whatever we ask—we know that we have what we asked of Him."[15]

Wow! Pretty simple, just ask according to His will. Too often however, we want to sift the will of God through a filter of how will this affect us. Our prayers reflect a notion that we are certain that we know God's will, and not only do we know His will, we also know the best way for His will to be accomplished.

Not long ago, I was having lunch with a friend. As I was about to leave, he asked me to pray for his daughter. I am not sure if it was because he knew that I had a daughter and I loved her very much or if he was just desperate. He shared with me how his daughter had been raised in the church, how she had committed her life to Christ at an early age, but how she had drifted from the church in recent years. She was living the life of a prodigal.

As I left, I assured him that I would pray for his little girl. I had a thirty-minute drive back to the office. Plenty of time to inform God of all the circumstances surrounding this situation and enough time to make my passionate plea for God to intervene and open her eyes and bring her to her senses. After all, I had a little girl. Surely, I knew how God should handle this problem. But before I began to pray, I decided to seek the Father's will. If I were to pray in earnest, if I wanted to pray a James 5:16 prayer, if I wanted to pray a prayer that would effectively change her life, then surely, I needed to pray a prayer in accordance with the Father's will.

So I cried out, "Oh God, how do I pray? What will have the biggest impact on her life right now?" And the Spirit of God revealed to me this is how you should pray. I pulled off to the side of the road and called my friend. I said here's how God wants me to pray for your daughter. The Holy Spirit said to me, "Pray the Father would bless her."

At first, I thought to myself, *She is living the life of a prodigal. She is living with a guy, and they aren't married. She hasn't been in church for a long time. She knows this is wrong. She knows that her mom and dad don't approve. She knows that she has broken their hearts. She knows that what she is doing is wrong in the eyes of God.*

And the Holy Spirit did not whisper. He did not stutter. All He said was "Pray the Father would bless her."

I realized that God the Father would never bless our sin. He would never bless our rebellion. He would never bless our rejection of His word and His Spirit. But Christ who loved the church and gave Himself up for her [before He could ever bless her—the church] would have to make her holy because there was nothing in her that was holy. He would cleanse her by the washing with water through His word because she could never cleanse herself. He would present her to Himself as a radiant church, without stain or winkle or any other blemish, but holy and blameless. He would do this Himself because she could never do it by herself.

I realized that only a love that was able to see beyond our sin, through the blood of Jesus, could ever bless a sinner like me.

After sharing with my friend what the Holy Spirit had revealed to me about how I should pray for his daughter, I said, "Before I let you go, can I ask you a question?"

He said, "Sure, you can ask me anything."

I said, "Does she know how much you love her?"

He said, "What?"

I said, "Does she know how much you lover her?"

There was an awkward moment of silence. I sensed that I might have struck a nerve. I knew my friend loved his little girl. She was his only child. He would do anything for her. There was nothing in life, except his wife, that he valued more than his daughter.

I said, "Don't misunderstand. I know you love her. I'm sure that you love her as much as I love my own daughter. But does she know how much you love her? If the last conversation you had with her was the last conversation you ever had with her, would she know her father's love? Would she feel blessed, or would she feel judged? Remember the day she was born, and you held her for the very first time. She took your breath away. Is that the love she feels today? Does she feel more love from her father, or does she feel more love from the world? I know you are disappointed. I know she has broken your heart. I am not saying that by loving her, you accept or approve of her lifestyle. That's not love. That's a lie from Satan. The world says, 'If you love me, you will accept me and embrace me. If not, then you must hate me.'"

The cross says, "I love you too much to leave you where you are". Jesus came to show the Father's love. He was cursed so that we might be blessed. He came to reconcile us with the Father so that the blessing we have lost would be restored. Don't let the world love her more than you do.

There are times when we need to pray for God to rebuke our children. There are times when we need to pray for God to love our children and bless them. But most of the time, we need to pray for God to give us the wisdom and grace to see our children as He sees them.

How many times have I prayed as if I were the self-appointed guardian of grace? I have prayed as if I know best when someone should receive mercy and grace and when someone should receive justice. Too often, we don't like it when the guilty go free. We want mercy for ourselves and maybe those we love, but we are appalled when the evildoers receive a pardon. We want justice. In our mind, there needs to be some retribution when the prodigal comes home. The father throws a party, and like the older son, we get angry. All we see is an undeserved blessing, and we don't like it.

Pray with the innocence of a child. Pray for God's unconditional blessing.

To be blessed by God is a good thing. To be blessed by God and know that you are blessed by God is a far greater thing. One of my favorite passages of scripture from the Old Testament is Genesis 1:27–28. "So God created man in His own image; in the image of God He created him; male and female He created them.[27] Then God blessed them, and God said to them, 'Be fruitful and multiply; fill the earth and subdue it; have dominion over the fish of the sea, over the birds of the air, and over every living thing that moves on the earth.'"[28]

As I read this familiar passage, a passage that I had read several times before, something had changed. Life was different now. My wife had been diagnosed with cancer.

Everything had changed. I had no problem accepting that man had been created in the image of God, but the only thing I saw as I read this day was the very first thing that God did after He created man. I had always focused on what God said to man in verse 28. I had never paid any attention to what God did for man.

God said to them, "Be fruitful and multiply; fill the earth and subdue it; have dominion over the fish of the sea, over the birds of the air, and over every living thing that moves on the earth."[28]

The words that spoke to me with great clarity and volume on this day was what God did for man after He created man in His image. "Then He blessed them."[28]

Don't miss that. The very first thing that God did for His children was to bless them. The God of all creation opened the windows of heaven and poured blessings upon blessings unto His children. At that point, it was beyond my finite mind to comprehend the depth of the meaning imbedded in those four words. From creation to the cross, from the cross to the grave, from death to resurrection, from Genesis to Revelation, the word of God reveals the blessings of God reserved for the children of God.

For just a moment, I wondered what the blessing of God might look like. I wanted to see the blessing. I wanted a glimpse of God's infinite blessing. I asked myself, "Who do I know that is blessed by God?" With my eyes closed, I tried to imagine what it would look like to be blessed by God.

In the stillness of that moment, the Spirit of God whispered in my ear that I was a child of God and that I was a picture of what the blessing of God looked like. Wow! I am a child of God. I am blessed by God. It's true. I honestly could not think of anyone more blessed than I was at that moment. My wife had cancer. The doctors had given us very little hope, but we were blessed. Not only did I feel blessed, I believed that she was blessed as well. We were greatly blessed. The one thing in our lives that the world said was a curse—*cancer*—had become one of our greatest blessings. To live like you are dying is a precious gift. Every day is a treasure.

The greatest blessing of God is the peace of God that comes from being at peace with God. The person who is most blessed is not the person with the most stuff; it is not the person with the least difficulties or trials. The person who is most blessed is the person that realizes that they are blessed.

For just a moment, I thought, If not me and if not her, then what would a picture of the blessing of God look like? My brother-in-law, Todd, was the only other person in my mind that came close to being as blessed as I was. He and my younger sister had recently lost their firstborn son. Todd's mother had been diagnosed with leukemia, and Todd's father was losing his eyesight. My sister and I had recently lost our father. Todd and my sister were struggling financially just to get by. Never getting ahead, they were just average people of average means. Why did I think he was blessed? According to the world, he was not blessed. He was far from it, and so was I.

What made me think that he was blessed? What made me think that we were blessed? I knew that in his mind, he knew that he was undeservedly blessed, and so was I.

Don't miss the rose because you fear the thorn.

Cancer is the thorn, but to live life every day to the fullest is a beautiful rose. To live your life as if each day is a precious gift is to appreciate the rose. To marvel at the beauty of the rising sun, to sit at the ocean's edge and watch the waves, and to gaze up into a sky so blue it almost hurts your eyes is to live your life, and to treasure the rose in spite of the thorns.

Embrace the rose.

Pray like a child for God's unconditional blessing!

6

PRAY BELIEVING THAT GOD IS THE ANSWER TO YOUR PRAYERS

It was lunchtime, but I wasn't really hungry. I decided to spend my lunch break praying for my wife. I locked the front door. I went into my office and closed the door. I opened my Bible to Matthew chapter six. "Don't be like the hypocrites.[5]When you pray, go into your room, close the door, and pray to your Father, who is unseen. Then your Father, who sees what is done in secret, will hear your prayer and He will answer your prayer.[6] Don't keep on babbling like the pagans.[7] Your Father knows what you need before you even ask."[8] Matthew 6: 5–8

We needed a miracle. The doctors had given us more bad news. We desperately needed a little hope, a little help, and some good news.

I needed to pray the perfect prayer. And Jesus said, "This is how you should pray."

I began to pray, "Our Father in heaven, we need you now. Please help us. For we have no power to face this enemy alone. We don't know what to do."

I thought that if I took the model prayer, and King Jehoshaphat's prayer from 2 Chronicles chapter twenty, and Hezekiah's prayer from 2 Kings chapter nineteen and mixed it all together, I could pray a prayer that would surely move God's heart.

"You, O Lord are the God of Israel. You alone are God over all the earth. You have made the heavens and the earth. Power and might are in Your hand. If calamity comes upon us, or plague or famine, we will stand in Your presence and cry out to You in our distress, and You will hear us and save us."

"Hallowed be thy Name. There is power in the name of Jesus. There is healing in the name of Jesus. Nothing is able to stand against that name. Even the demons tremble at the name of Jesus. Cancer has no power against the name of Jesus. It is the name that is above all names. There is no other name under heaven given among men by which we must be saved. Whatever you ask in My Name, this I will do, that the

Father may be glorified in the Son. For everyone who calls upon the name of the Lord will be saved."

"Your kingdom come. Your will be done on earth as it is in heaven. You rule the nations. The heavens are Yours. If the kingdoms of this world cannot stand against Your will, then whom shall I fear? If You have defeated every enemy, then why should I worry? You and You alone defeated Sennacherib, King of Assyria, when the Assyrians came against Hezekiah. You and You alone, O' Lord, defeated the Moabites and the Ammonites and the Meunites which came to make war against Jehoshaphat and all those who lived in Judah and Jerusalem. Will You not defend us against this relentless enemy that continues to attack us? Will You not rescue us? We have no power to stand against cancer without You. We don't know what to do. We turn our eyes toward You. Deliver us O' Lord from the grip of our enemy. Heal Debbie from this cancer that is waging war against her body. Do what only You can do and what the doctors cannot do so that everyone will know that You alone are God. And we will praise Your name. We will testify to Your goodness forever."

I was on a roll! This prayer rocked! "Give us this day our daily bread." And that was as far as I got.

I'm praying for healing. I'm praying against cancer. I am praying for a miracle. I don't need daily bread. I can feed myself. I can provide for my family. We weren't hungry. We needed healing. We needed a miracle, and a miracle is what I got.

It was as if Christ was standing in front me with His arms stretched open wide. I said, "Give us this day our daily bread." He said, "My grace is sufficient for this day. My power is sufficient for this day. My comfort is sufficient for this day. My provision is sufficient for this day. My help is sufficient for this day. My hope is sufficient for this day. My presence is sufficient for this day. My good news is sufficient for this day. My peace is sufficient for this day. My healing is sufficient for this day."

He said, "Don't worry about tomorrow. Instead, seek first My kingdom and My righteousness because I am able to supply every need according to My riches. Tomorrow will have enough trouble of its own. But the good news is, like today, I will be enough for tomorrow. My grace will be sufficient tomorrow. My power will be sufficient tomorrow. My comfort will be sufficient tomorrow. My help will be sufficient tomorrow. My hope will be sufficient tomorrow. My presence will be sufficient tomorrow. Don't worry about tomorrow. This is the day that the Lord has made. What if tomorrow never comes? What if today is all you have?"

Embrace this day. Rejoice this day. Dance today. Sing today. Smile today. Laugh today.

Whatever the need, remember this:

He is sufficient for this day.

He said, "My healing is sufficient for this day."

Little children live in the moment.

Pray like a child. Pray in the moment.

7

SAY A LITTLE PRAYER FOR ME

It was a Wednesday morning, July 31, 2013. I went to see Jason, my son. He needed to borrow some money. He had a court appearance that afternoon, and he was twenty dollars short. We talked about life, the weather, and guy stuff. Then I handed him a twenty-dollar bill. He hugged my neck and said, "Thanks, Dad."

I said, "I love you, bud."

He said, "I love you, Dad."

As I turned and began walking to my car, he said something that I'll never forget. He said, "Say a little prayer for me today."

I stopped. I turned around, and I looked him square in the eyes. I said, "I always pray for you, bud. But there is nothing little or trivial about it."

I know that he did not mean to imply that prayer is a trivial pursuit, something we do when it is convenient. But sometimes our words imply something different than what we really mean, and sometimes they reveal how we really feel. Say a little prayer for me. Prayers would be appreciated. Really? Do we believe that a little prayer offered on the altar of convenience, at a time of our choosing, when we have nothing else to do will make a difference?

Who told us that a James 5:16 prayer is a little prayer? The effective fervent prayer of a righteous man accomplishes much. The prayer offered for healing is no little prayer. The prayer that moves mountains and breaks down strongholds is no trivial prayer. A prayer that restores a broken marriage is no little prayer. A prayer for a prodigal child is no little prayer. No prayer is little in the eyes of God. The size of your prayer does not determine how important your petition is to God. God is not moved by the length of your prayer or the eloquence of your speech. The size of your prayer is not nearly as important as the size of your God. Your position in prayer is more important than your petition. The position of a righteous man whose prayer accomplishes much is not whether he kneels or stands.

It doesn't matter if his head is bowed or his eyes are closed or if his hands are raised or folded. The position that matters, as you offer your petition, is to make sure that you are in the presence of a holy God. The petition offered on holy ground is always heard.

Luke 22:44 says that Christ, being in anguish, prayed more earnestly, and His sweat was like drops of blood falling to the ground. When the beloved Son prayed to God the Father, there was nothing little or trivial about it. Never before had a more righteous man, positioned on holy ground, offered a more fervent prayer to a more loving Father. Yet even so, God did not deliver Him. God did not rescue Him. God the Father did not save Him. God the Father did not ignore the Son. He heard the prayer of His only Son. God sent a messenger. An angel appeared to Him and strengthened Him.

In the seventeenth chapter of John, there is nothing little or trivial about Christ's prayer. He prayed for Himself. Then He prayed for His disciples. Then He prayed for you and me and all who would come to a saving faith in Him. It was a simple prayer for protection and sanctification. It was simple but not little or trivial.

Luke 5:16 says that Jesus often withdrew to solitary places to pray. He positioned Himself in the presence of the Father. He positioned Himself away from the distractions of the world to be alone with the Father. There was nothing trivial about the time He spent with the Father.

Luke 6:12 says that on one day, Jesus went out to the hills to pray and spent the night praying to God. Again, He positioned Himself in the presence of the Father. And He spent the night with the Father, just talking about stuff. And it was good because time spent with the Father is never insignificant or trivial.

When we pray and petition to God, do we consider our position? Do we offer our prayers on holy ground? Or have we become so good at multitasking that we pray while checking our e-mail or updating our status on Facebook? Do we pray while listening to our favorite tunes and doing our morning workout? Do we pray while riding the bike or running down the highway? Do we offer little prayers and wonder why there is very little that changes? Do we consider our position before we offer our petition? Do we pray like it matters, or has prayer become so routine that we just go through the motions?

After Jason and I talked some more about prayer and how God the Father views the time we spend in prayer, I prayed for him. I prayed with him, and I prayed over him. I hugged his neck again.

He said, "I love you, Dad."

I said, "I love you, bud."

Neither of us had any idea that would be the last time we would talk, embrace, hug each other's neck, and say, "I love you man." Two days later, he was involved in an automobile accident that took his life.

If you ask me to pray for you, I will. If you ask me to say a "little prayer" for you, we will probably talk first; then I'll pray for you.

Don't pray little prayers. Pray big prayers!

Little children pray big prayers.

They may not use big words, but they always pray to a big God.

8

PRAY THAT GOD WOULD SPEAK

Just before Debbie died, her mother was placed in a nursing home. The reality that her baby girl was not doing well had a devastating effect on the health of my mother-in-law. Her ninety-year old body was weak and worn from the years of caring for her paraplegic husband. It broke her heart to see her little girl sick. Near the end, Debbie was no longer able to go to the nursing home to visit her mother. They would talk on the phone, and Debbie would ask me to go to the nursing home and pray over her mother, and I would.

After Debbie died, I continued to go to the nursing home a couple of times every week just to pray over and to pray with my mother-in-law. One Sunday afternoon, I arrived, and she was sleeping. I wanted to pray for her, but I did not want to disturb her. I knew she needed her rest. For over two weeks, she had been unable to get out of bed without assistance. She was becoming discouraged; her body was growing weaker. As I stood at the foot of her bed, I thought about the life she had lived. I wanted desperately to pray a James 5:16 prayer over her. I wanted to pray a prayer that mattered. I wanted to pray a prayer that would make a difference. But the reality was that she would probably never leave the nursing home. This was where she would die. She would probably never get out of the bed again without assistance. She would not walk the halls anymore. She would never go outside and see the blue sky or feel the breeze upon her face again.

Without opening my mouth, without making a sound, I cried out in my spirit, Oh God, how do I pray for this sweet lady? And the Holy Spirit spoke to me with a clarity that was overwhelming. It was as if I were standing on holy ground, and the Word that I received was simple and profound. It was simply profound.

"Just pray the Father would speak to her." That was all. Just pray the Father would speak to her. Because if God said, "Get up and walk, my child," she would rise and walk. If God said, "Well done, my child. Well done. You have been faithful. Come and take your rest. Enjoy the inheritance prepared for you." That might be even better if God said, "Well done. Well done."

So I prayed that God would speak to her because the Word of God is:

- hope for the hopeless

- strength for the weak

- salvation for the lost

- healing for the sick

- restoration for the broken

- comfort for the hurting

- peace in the midst of the chaos

- a lamp onto our feet

- a shining light in the darkness

- food for a hungry soul

- rest for the weary

- alive

- without fault

- enduring forever

When my God speaks:

- the mountains move

- strongholds will come down

- the enemy will flee

- the blind will see

- the lame will walk

- the dumb will talk

- the deaf will hear

- the weak will rule

- the strong will serve

- the simple things will amaze us all

- tears will cease

- cancer will die

- the lonely will sing

- the rejected will rejoice

- the brokenhearted will dance with joy

- death will die

- there will be no more goodbyes

- babies won't die

- mothers won't cry

- daddies won't leave

- demons will shake and tremble with fear

- the proud will fall

- the meek will rise

- the last will be first

- the hungry will eat as much as they want

- the rejected of men will sit with the King

Sometimes we just need to pray that God would speak and that we would have ears to hear.

In the beginning, before the foundation of the world had been laid out, God spoke. He opened His mouth to speak, and what was not became what is by the Word of God.

He said, "Let there be light," and there was light. He said, "Let there be an expanse between the waters to separate water from water," and it was so. He said, "Let the water under the sky be gathered to one place, and let dry ground appear," and it was so. He said, "Let the land produce vegetation: seed-bearing plants and trees on the land that bear fruit with seed in it, according to their various kind," and it was so. He said, "Let there be light in the expanse of the sky to separate the day from the night," and it was so. He said, "Let the water teem with living creatures, and let birds fly above the earth," and it was so. He said, "Let the land produce living creatures according to their kind," and it was so. He said, "Let us make man in our image, in our likeness, and let them rule over the fish of the sea, the birds of the air, and over all the creatures that move along the ground," and it was so.

The Word of God created all things. In the beginning was the Word, and the Word was with God, and the Word was God.[1] He was with God in the beginning.[2] Through Him all things were made: without Him nothing was made that has been made.[3] John 1:1–3

The Word of God sustains all things. The Son is the radiance of God's glory and the exact representation of His Being, sustaining all things by His powerful Word. Hebrews 1:3

Jesus answered, "It is written: Man shall not live on bread alone, but on every word that comes from the mouth of God." Mathew 4:4

One evening as I was praying for my wife, I asked God to heal my knee. Runners can be difficult to live with when they are plagued with an injury that prevents them from running. I explained to God, as if He didn't already know, my knee injury was just a small matter compared to cancer. I knew He could speak a word and heal my knee. Even the centurion, in the eighth chapter of Matthew, knew the power of the word when God spoke. He said, "Lord, I do not deserve to have You come under my roof. But just say the word and my servant will be healed."[8]

Jesus was astonished by the faith of the centurion. He said to the centurion, "Go! It will be done just as you believed it would." And his servant was healed at that very hour.[13]

Before I could finish explaining to God that I realized He was obviously dealing with many more significant matters than my knee pain, He spoke. He didn't speak with a deep voice from some lofty place where He ruled and reigned. He spoke through His Spirit with a clarity as real as if He were standing right next to me. He said, "I will heal your knee if you will just walk."

I wish I could say that I accepted His word without question, like the centurion, and that my knee was healed at the very moment. I wish that I could say that, but I can't.

My initial response was "What? I am a runner. I am not a walker. I do not like admitting this, but I did not want to become a walker. I would occasionally get upset when someone said they had seen me jogging. How would I cope if someone said, "I saw you walking the other day." I wasn't a jogger. I wasn't a walker. I was a runner. And I could tolerate a little pain when I ran, but the truth was, the pain was getting worse. Throughout the day, I would have a sharp-shooting painful sensation from my knee all the way up to my lower back, and these painful sensations were getting worse and more frequent. So with a hint of pride, I began to explain to God why I really didn't want to be a walker.

I can only imagine how God must have rolled His eyes as I continued to explain the situation, hoping that He would see things from my point of view.

Then He spoke again, "I will heal your knee if you will just walk."

With a bit of reservation, I decided to test God. I knew that His word would not return void. It says so in the Book of Isaiah, "So shall My word be that goes forth from My mouth; it shall not return to Me void. But it shall accomplish what I please. And it shall prosper in the thing for which I sent it." Isaiah 55:11

The following morning, I decided, no more running. I would walk, for a little while. Prior to this day, every morning, Debbie would walk through the neighborhood as I ran. After I had run my five miles, I would find her, and we would walk back home together. She stayed within one block of the house, so we were never more than half a mile from the house when I would meet up with her. But this morning was different. We started together, and we walked together, and it was good. For several months, we walked together every morning. We would hold hands like we were eighteen. I would tell her to close her eyes as she held my hand. I would say, "Just breathe and believe. Believe that the breeze in your face is the very breath of God. Believe that God is going to heal you. Believe that God is preparing you to do great work for His kingdom. Believe that you will share your story with many, and many lives will be touched by you. Just breathe and believe, baby." One morning after we had walked, she was in the bathroom. I was getting dressed. She lost her balance and fell. She broke her ankle in two spots. The X-rays and MRI (magnetic resonance imaging) results that followed revealed it was worse than just a broken ankle. The cancer had spread, and it had spread to her brain.

For the next five months, we didn't walk. I pushed her every morning in her wheelchair through the neighborhood. We would hold hands like we were eighteen. I would tell her to close her eyes as she held my hand. I would say, "Just breathe and believe, baby. Believe that the breeze in your face is the very breath of God. Believe that God is going to heal you. Believe that God is preparing you to do great work for His kingdom. Believe that you will share your story with many and that many lives will be touched by you. Just breathe and believe, baby."

On Christmas Eve, I pushed her through the neighborhood, and we looked at Christmas lights. On January 18, 2007, God took her.

It was cold and windy the day of her funeral. Darkness came early that evening. I wanted to run. I wanted to put on my running shoes and run again. I thought that if I could run, maybe I could just run away. It was dark and cold, and I was alone. I went to the community center where there was a lighted running path. I didn't care if it hurt. No pain could compare to the pain I felt. As I got out of my car, I saw two young girls in the distance. One appeared to be injured. I walked over to see if I could help. They were cross-country runners, and one of them had twisted her ankle badly. She couldn't walk. I offered to carry her to her car.

She looked up at me and said, "You can't do that."

As I picked her up, I said, "For the last five months, I have carried my wife because she couldn't walk. Earlier today, I carried her for the last time. I walked her home. I think I'm here for a reason. I'm supposed to do this for you."

I carried her to her car. After she and her friend drove off, I looked up into the sky and said, "I'm going to run now." And I did, without pain. God had healed my knee. It had nothing to do with whether I was a walker or a runner. It was all about her. And it was about me being where I was supposed to be, walking beside her for the rest of her life.

I thought God was preparing her for kingdom work, but God was preparing her for the kingdom. I got to walk her home. That's when I realized that He was preparing me for kingdom work.

I am the one who will tell her story and give God the glory.

If God gives you a word, stand on it.

If you don't know what to pray, pray that God would speak.

It has been said that a child can recognize its mother's voice even in the womb.

When you pray, be like a child. Ask God to speak and pray that you will recognize His voice.

9

PRAY TO GOD LIKE HE IS THERE

How many times have I prayed, and even shed a tear, but wondered if my prayer had reached the ear of God? How could my prayer possibly reach the throne room of an almighty God if it never went any higher than the ceiling? Was it me? Was there something hindering my prayers from ascending to the heavenly realm? Did I have unclean hands or an impure heart? Were my motives out of line? Was there unconfessed sin that robbed my prayers of the power to rise and break through the ceiling above my head? Or was I praying to a God who was so distant that I could not reach Him regardless of how passionate my plea or how loud I cried? Was I praying to a God who was sitting on His throne in the high places of heaven, ruling and reigning from afar?

Our Father who art in heaven, I know you are out there somewhere. I want to believe you can hear me when I pray. Sometimes I gaze up into the heavens, looking for a sign that God is there. I know He is up there somewhere. After the resurrection, He appeared to the disciples. When He had led them out to the vicinity of Bethany, He lifted His hands and blessed them. While He was blessing them, He left them and was taken up into heaven. Luke 24:50–51

After the Lord Jesus had spoken to them, He was taken up into heaven, and He sat down at the right hand of God the Father. Mark 16:19

Even Stephen, as he was being stoned, looked up into heaven and saw the Son of Man standing at the right hand of God the Father. Acts 7:56

He's up there somewhere. I know He is. I just don't know what I have to do to be heard. Sometimes, I feel the need to go where He is to pray. If I go to His church and pray, surely, He will hear my prayer. He is there. It's His church, and He is always there. He said it Himself, "My house will be called a house of prayer." Matthew 21:13

Shortly before Debbie died, I remember thinking one Sunday morning if I could somehow manage to get her to church this morning. At the end of the service, we could go to the altar. In the Father's house, on hallowed ground, we could cry out. God's people would gather around us, and together in unison and in one accord, we could pray to God. We would know that He heard our prayers because He was there.

She was weak, too weak to even go to church. I stayed home with her that Sunday morning. We had church there in our living room. We prayed right there. Church is not a building. Church is where God is. He was there. Christ told the disciples. "Surely, I will be with you always, even to the very end of the age." Matthew 28:20

Jesus said the same thing in John's gospel. "And I will ask the Father, and He will give you another [comforter, counselor, the Spirit of truth, the Holy Spirit, the third person of the Trinity] to be with you forever." John 14:16

"Where two or three are gathered in My name, I will be there with them." Matthew 18:20

He was there. He heard our prayers.

If He is with us always through the indwelling of the Holy Spirit, if He is here right now, then why would I need to go somewhere else to pray? Three days later, on Wednesday evening just after we had eaten supper, there was a knock at the door. I opened the door, and there stood four friends. One of them said, "We are the church, and we have come to pray for your wife." We all went into the living room where Debbie was resting on the couch. We gathered around her and prayed, and because God was there, He heard our prayers.

If He is with me always, then He must be with me even now. He must be right here, right now.

When you pray, you can pray to God the Father, Jehovah Shammah, "The Lord who is there." He is there in His church. He is there in your room. He is there at the foot of your bed. He is there when you go out and when you come in. He is there. Just talk to Him like He is there.

He was there with Daniel in the lion's den. He was there with Elijah as he hid in a cave at Horeb on the mountain. He was there with Hagar in the desert when she ran away from Sarai. He was there with Shadrach, Meshach, and Abednego in the fiery furnace. He was there with Moses when he led the Israelites out of Egypt. He was there with Elisha in Dothan when the king of Aram sent his army to surround the city. He was there with Jonah when he spent three days in the belly of the whale.

He has always been there. Just because we may not see Him does not mean He isn't there. He is always there.

As I was eating breakfast alone one day last week, I remembered the first time I ate breakfast alone after Debbie died. I looked at the empty chair across from me, and I cried. Many times, I have eaten alone and cried as I stared at the empty chair. I did not cry today, but the prevailing question on my mind today was, "Where was God?" Where was God in the garden when the serpent deceived Eve? Where was God when Cain killed Abel? Where was God when my wife died? Was He there? And where was God when my son died?

Two days ago, a fellow cyclist was killed when he was struck by a car while he was riding his bike on a stretch of road that I ride all the time. Where was God two days ago? Was He there with my friend?

I had more questions than answers that morning.

As I finished my coffee, I looked at the empty chair across from me one more time. It was a chair that did not use to be empty. I asked myself, "Is God there?"

Walking to my car, I noticed a young man standing next to his vehicle. The door was opened and the hood raised. As I got closer, I saw a young girl sitting in the grass. My first inclination was to see if I could help. My second inclination was that's dumb. I am not a mechanic. I don't know anything about cars. As dumb as it was, I said, "I'm not a mechanic, but is there anything I can do?"

His response was unexpected to say the least, but then God doesn't always do what we expect. The young man said, "You don't have any water, do you?"

I had just walked out of Cracker Barrel. I had nothing in my hands. I smiled, and I said, "The odds of me having water with me are one in a million, but as a matter of fact, I do." There were three bottles of water in the floorboard of my car. They had been there since Jax, my grandson, and I had gone floating down the Spring River over the weekend. Up until that moment, I thought I had been eating breakfast alone that morning.

I saw an empty chair, but I AM was there!

Sometimes, I think we forget that before the cross, in the Old Testament, God's people were under the old covenant. There was a veil that separated us from the presence of God.

Isaiah prophesied in the Old Testament that there would be a day when God would come to dwell with men. "Therefore, the Lord Himself will give you a sign: Behold, a virgin will be with child and bear a son, and she will call His name Immanuel." Isaiah 7:14

Immanuel, God with us. There would be a day when God would leave heaven and come to earth to dwell with men, but that day had not yet come. Then one day, an angel of the Lord appeared to some shepherds during the night and said, "I bring you good news of great joy that will be for all the people. Today in the town of David, it happened just like God said it would! A Savior has been born to you. He is the prophesied One. He is Christ Jesus, the Lord Immanuel."

From that day on, God dwelt among men. Immanuel, God was with man up until that dark appointed hour. When on an old rugged cross at the edge of town, between two thieves, Immanuel was crucified. It happened just like He said it would. But before it happened, He told them not to be troubled by what was about to take place. He said, "I will ask the Father, and He will give you another Counselor, to be with you forever—the Spirit of Truth. The world will not accept Him, because it neither sees Him nor knows Him. But you know Him, because He will live with you and will be in you." John 14: 16–17

When Jesus had cried out again in a loud voice, He gave up His spirit. At that moment, the curtain of the temple was torn in two from top to bottom. The earth shook, and the rocks split. And there was no longer any distinction between the empty chair and the throne of grace.

He is there on the throne of grace.

He is also there in the empty chair.

Pray like a child who talks with a friend in the empty chair.

He occupies the empty space when we call His name and seek His face.

He occupies the empty chair when the one we love is no longer there.

10

PRAY SIMPLE PRAYERS

Have you ever listened to a child pray? They tend to pray simple prayers as compared to the prayer of most adults. Maybe that's because things just aren't as complicated when you are three years old. For the most part, you are totally dependent upon someone else to provide food, shelter, and clothing. If you want something, you ask for it. If a child wants a piece of cake, they will simply say, "I want a piece of cake." If a child asks God for something in prayer, it is usually just as simple and direct.

It gets a little more complicated though if Mom wants a piece of cake. Before Mom asks for a piece of cake, she thinks to herself about the price to be paid. Even though I really would like a piece of cake, I don't need a piece of cake. I really need to lose a couple of pounds. I'll gain five pounds if I eat that piece of cake. Maybe I should just have an apple instead or some carrot sticks. Chocolate cake is my favorite. I'll skip breakfast tomorrow and have a piece of cake tonight, or maybe I'll eat two pieces. I could spend an extra fifteen minutes on the treadmill. Who am I kidding? I'm not going to spend five minutes on the treadmill. Why is it that everything that tastes good, like cake and ice cream and mashed potatoes and biscuits and gravy and fried chicken and sweet tea, is bad for you? I just want some chocolate cake.

Finally, Mom decides to ask for a piece of cake. She says, "I would like a piece of cake please. I don't want an outside piece. I prefer a piece from the center of the cake without all the icing. Could you make it a small piece and bring me a small dish of vanilla ice cream with hot fudge syrup, whipped cream, and a cherry on top."

And so it is when Mom asks God for something in prayer. Our prayers get more complicated as we get older. We feel the need to rationalize, justify, and even defend our request. We are more concerned with how to frame our request than we are with simply asking for help. We no longer want to pray simple prayers. We want to offer our request in such a way that God will be moved to act because we have obviously put a great deal of effort in framing our prayer.

Maybe that is what the disciples had in mind when they asked Jesus to teach them how to pray.

In Luke 11:1, the disciples wanted to know how to frame their prayers so that they could be assured of a positive response. They wanted to know the secret to praying effective prayers. Surely, Jesus could tell them something that would give them an advantage over everyone else.

You might think based upon the volumes that have been written on the subject of prayer that Jesus's answer should have taken at least one full chapter, maybe even two full chapters to cover just the basics of an acceptable prayer. A simple online search or a quick visit to your local Christian bookstore will yield over one hundred thousand titles on the subject of prayer.

There are books that teach us how to pray:

- With Awe and Intimacy for God

- Specific, Serious and Strategic Prayers

- From Basic Prayers to Targeted Strategies

- Prayers That Will Make a Difference

- Prayers That Connect Us to God

- Prayers of Intercession

- Like a Powerful Prayer Warrior

- For 40 Days

- The 31 Powerful Prayers

- The Essentials of Prayer

- Prayers That Rout Demons

- Methods of Prayer That Will Change Your Life

- Prayers for Hard Times

- Morning Prayers

- Prayers That Move Mountains

- Prayers of Protection

- Prayers for Healing

- Prayers That Bring Calm and Peace

- Prayers for Men

- Prayers for Women

- Prayers for Faith

- Prayers for Hope

- Prayers for Every Struggle

- Prayers for Bearing Fruit

- The ABCs of Prayer

- Prayers Specifically for Prodigals

- Contemplative Prayers

- According to God's Will

- For Miracles

- With Boldness

- For Peace

Jesus responded in a way that even a child could understand. His answer was simple and to the point. He said to them, "When you pray, say: Father." Then He took three verses and taught them how to pray. Luke 11:2–4

It reminds me of the time I asked an expert for advice about running. I had been a runner all my life, but I never entered a race until after my wife died. I never owned a Garmin. I never knew how fast I was. I didn't know what my resting heart rate was or how it compared to my heart rate during aerobic activity. Stride length, cadence, and pace per mile meant nothing to me. I ran for fitness, and I ran for fun. At the age of fifty-three, I decided one day that I would run a marathon. All I knew was that a marathon was 26.2 miles, and I was currently running five miles per day, five or six times per week. My plan was simple. I would gradually increase my mileage on Tuesdays and Saturdays until I reached a point that I was able to run 26.2 miles without stopping. For three months, everything went according to schedule until one morning as I was within two miles of my house, I pulled a hamstring. No tears, nothing serious, it was just a minor setback. Within four weeks, I was gradually adding mileage again. By the middle of the summer, I was ready. I registered to run the Lewis and Clark Marathon. I still had no clue about heart rate, aerobic activity, stride length, cadence, or pace per mile; but I could do the distance. I had successfully run twenty-six miles on six different occasions that summer. As I was leaving town the day before the race, I stopped by the post office to mail a package. Standing in line in front of me was Ethan Busby. Ethan was my insurance agent, and he just happened to be a running icon in the local community. I never had the opportunity to run with him or even discuss running with him up to that point. As we stood there in line, I told him that I was going out of town to run my first race, a marathon. I asked if he could give me any advice.

Much like the disciples must have felt when they asked Jesus to teach them to pray, I anticipated that he might share some closely guarded secret that only the elite were privileged to. He was a running legend. Surely, from the depth of his knowledge, he could give me some priceless bit of information that would give me an advantage over everyone else.

He looked at me and said, "Have fun."

I said, "What?"

He said, "Have fun."

How much more simple could it be? He did not complicate things by talking about heart rate, aerobic activity, stride length, cadence, or pace per mile. He said to have fun.

When Christ answered the disciples after they had asked Him to teach them how to pray, His response was simple. He did not complicate things. Luke 11:2–4

He said, "Consider who you are talking to." Hallowed be Your name. You are my King. Volumes have been written about the kingship of God and the Kingdom of God. That simple statement says much about who God is. He is not only a king. He is not only my king. He is the King of kings. He is the Lord of lords and so much more. Jesus said, "Say Father." He said to consider who you are talking to and do not forget who you are. You are a child of the King. He said, "Say Father."

He said, "Make your request." Give us each day our daily bread. If you need a more comprehensive analysis of this concept, go back and review chapter 6: "Pray Believing That God Is the Answer to Your Prayer." He is sufficient for this day.

He said, "Confess your need." Forgive us our sins as we forgive others. It's all about grace, His grace. The unmerited gift of God. There is no such thing as "works righteousness." We receive grace, but that does not make us the guardians of grace. We extend His grace as He has extended it to us.

He said, "Then follow the Father." Lead us, and we could stop right there. Lead us not into temptation. Lead us away from temptation. Lead us in the paths of righteousness. Lead us beside the still waters. It's not about where He leads or doesn't lead. It's about us following.

Did Christ really expect us to pray simple prayers? How effective will we be if we pray simple prayers? Will a simple prayer really accomplish anything? Can we expect a simple prayer to move a mountain or break down a stronghold or rescue the prodigal child? Will a simple payer restore a marriage or set the captive free? Is the effective fervent prayer of a righteous man a simple thing, or is it a complicated thing?

We know that the effective fervent prayer of a righteous man is a prayer that accomplishes much. A prayer that accomplishes much is the kind of prayer we all want to pray. Sometimes we think if we frame our words just right and if we make our petitions in certain way, then God will be moved to action by our oratory skill, the eloquence of our words, and the articulation of our request. Then we will have surely prayed an effective prayer.

God is not impressed with the number of our words, our oratory skill, our command of the English language, or even our grammatical correctness. It doesn't matter how we frame our petition. According to Romans 8:26, when we, in our weakest moments, don't even know what we ought to pray, when we can't find the words, the Holy Spirit intercedes for us with groans that words cannot express and only the Father can understand.

Of all the sermons I've heard in my lifetime, there have been two that made an indelible mark and had a lasting impact. One was on the subject of the security of the believer. The other was on the subject of prayer. I think the simplicity of both messages, as they approached complex doctrinal issues of faith, is what resonated with me and has had a lasting impact upon my life. Dr. Rodney Reeves— who had served as chairman of the department of religion and philosophy and associate professor of religion at Williams Baptist College, Walnut Ridge, Arkansas—delivered the message on prayer that I'll never forget. In my opinion, Dr. Reeves was a great teaching pastor. He had the ability to take deep doctrinal subjects of faith and present them in a way that even a fifth grader could grasp with clarity and understanding. I don't recall the scripture passage that morning. I couldn't tell you what songs we sang. To be honest, I don't remember too much about that morning. But what I do remember is the simplicity of his message.

He said, "The older I get, the simpler my prayers become. Sometimes I just cry out, 'Lord, help me. Help me!'"

When Peter got down out of the boat and walked on the water toward Jesus, he took his eyes off Christ for just a moment. He saw the wind and the waves, and he was afraid, and he began to sink. He cried out, "Lord, save me!" It was just a simple prayer.

At that moment, Peter didn't feel the need to explain the situation to Jesus. There was no time to craft an eloquent prayer in hope that God would be moved to action by his oratory skills. Peter was desperate. Peter did not pray, "Dear Lord Jesus, the maker of heaven and earth, the God of Abraham, Isaac, and Jacob, You alone are God. You alone are worthy to be praised. You told me not to be afraid. You commanded me to step out of the boat and come to you. I did what you said. I was obedient. I stepped out, but now I'm beginning to sink. Things aren't working out the way I thought they would. I look around, and all I see is the storm. The wind and the waves are pulling me under. I didn't see this coming. If I could go back, maybe I would just stay in the boat. I must have been mistaken. Surely, I would not be in this mess if You had really commanded me to step out, but here we are. I need You now. I cannot save myself. Please rescue me, O Lord."

No! Peter prayed a simple prayer. Peter cried out, "Lord, save me!" In the blink of an eye, immediately Jesus reached out His hand to catch Peter.

Another time, a tax collector stood at a distance. He would not even look up to heaven, but he beat his chest and said, "God, have mercy on me, a sinner." It was just a simple prayer. By contrast, the self-righteous Pharisee stood up and prayed what he thought was a more eloquent prayer. He expressed gratitude for not being a desperate man with a desperate need. He was genuinely grateful that he was not like the tax collector or other evil men. He was neither desperate nor humble. He was obviously arrogant, self-righteous, and confident that his prayer would be heard because of his many words. Jesus responded by saying, "The simple prayer of the desperate tax collector offered in humility was acknowledged by God, but the prayer of the Pharisee was not."

When Debbie was first diagnosed with cancer, several members of our congregation stayed after service one Sunday evening to pray over her. Of all the prayers that were prayed that night and of all the prayers that were prayed from that point on, I remember one.

A dear friend cried out that night, "Lord, heal Debbie. Please heal Debbie!"

That was all. That was his prayer. And that was enough!

Who told us that God is moved by our oratory skills? Who told us that God is moved by the number of our words? Who told us that God is moved by the eloquence of our speech? Who told us that God is moved by the articulation of our request? Who told us that God is concerned with our grammatical correctness?

Pray simple prayers.

Pray like a child asking for a piece of cake.

If you are having trouble with praying simple prayers, ask a child to teach you how to pray.

11

PRAY BELIEVING THAT HE KNOWS YOUR NEED

Would it change the way you prayed if you knew that God knew what you needed before you even asked? What if He not only knew what you needed but He also knew what you were going to ask for before you even began to pray? Jesus told the disciples not to be like the pagans when they prayed. There was no need to keep on babbling. He said, "Using many words to make your point is not necessary because God the Father knows what you need before you even ask." Not only does He know what you need, He knows what you will ask before you begin to pray. "Before a word is on my tongue, You know it completely, O Lord." Psalms 139:4

He knows everything about you. He knows the number of your days. "Your eyes saw my unformed body. All the days ordained for me were written in Your book before one of them came to be." Psalm 139:16

Even the very hairs of your head are all numbered. Matthew 10:30

If He has numbered the hairs of your head, if He knows the number of your days, if He has determined the number of stars in the sky and calls each one by name, is there anything hidden from Him? Is there anything He does not know?

A group of researchers at the University of Hawaii, who were somewhat acquainted with sandy beaches, set out to calculate the number of grains of sand on earth. They assumed that if all the grains of sand were approximately consistent in size, you could calculate how many grains of sand are in a teaspoon and then multiply that number by the area of all the beaches and deserts in the world. Based upon their calculations, the earth has approximately seven and a half quintillion grains of sand (7.5 x 1018).

That's a lot of sand. But how does that compare to the number of stars in the sky? We don't know for sure because we don't know for sure how many stars there are. We don't know for sure how many grains of sand there are either. No man has ever counted either of them. The Hubble Space Telescope has, however, revealed things in recent years that are almost unfathomable. Some scientists estimate that the number of stars in our galaxy alone, the Milky Way Galaxy, to be roughly one hundred billion. Other estimates put that number as high as two hundred billion. Some scientists estimate the number of galaxies like our galaxy could be as high as ten trillion; others put the number closer to one hundred billion. Multiply the number of galaxies by one hundred billion stars in each galaxy and you get a really big number. Most astronomers put current estimates of the total number of stars in the observable universe at roughly seventy sextillion (7×10^{22}). That's a big, big number, and it's just a guess. The actual number is known by God. But get this: He doesn't just know the number; He calls each star by name (Psalm 147:4).

It occurred to me as I was praying for a friend that it was not necessary for me to inform God of my friend's situation. God was fully aware of the circumstances. Did I really think that this might come as a surprise to God? He not only knew the circumstance of my friend's situation; He knew a lot more than I did. God already knew how this happened. He knew why this was happening. He knew when it started. God didn't need me to bring Him up to speed. And God certainly didn't need me to tell Him how to fix the problem. But how many times have I asked God for a blessing, and in my mind's eye, I held a picture of what that blessing would look like? The measuring rod, by which I would determine whether God had heard my request and answered my prayer, would be if the blessing were received as I had pictured it before I even began to pray.

God never intended for me to have the answers before I came to Him in prayer. Paul tells us in Romans 8:26–27 that when we don't even know what we ought to pray in our weakness, the Spirit will help us. He will intercede for us with groans that words cannot even express. And God the Father, who searches our hearts, knows the mind of the Spirit. And the Spirit always intercedes for the saints according to the will of God the Father. I don't have to know where we are going or how we are going to get there. I just have to be willing to follow God.

Many times have I set out to follow God and I end up going in a different direction. There have been times that I have prayed early in the morning because I knew the day ahead would be filled with challenges and difficulties. I would bring my calendar and my to-do list into my prayer room. I would lay it out before God. I explained to God the importance of accomplishing each and every task that I was facing that day. I confessed my dependence upon Him. I acknowledged that unless He led me that day, I would have no confidence in my own ability to complete the tasks. I would desperately plead for God to lead me.

After a quick shower and a cup of coffee, I would charge out the front door, confident that nothing would be able to hinder my success. I had spent time with God first thing this morning. I was going to follow Him. He was out in front. He had the lead, and He knew where we were going. I had outlined to Him in great details my agenda for the day. What could possibly go wrong?

I don't know, but something obviously has. It's early in the day, and I am already concerned things are not going the way I had planned. Something is wrong, and I'm not quite sure what it is. I thought all I have to do is follow God, and everything will be okay. By the end of the day, I am angry, frustrated, and disappointed. After supper, I go into my study and begin to pray. I ask God, "What happened? Where were You? Why did You not lead me today?"

All God said was "Why did you not follow me? I went right, and you went left. You had a plan. I had a better plan."

I wanted to follow God, but I wanted Him to lead where I wanted to go. It didn't occur to me that He might have a different plan, a better plan.

Jesus said it Himself, "Your Father knows what you need before you even ask Him." Matthew 6:8

Don't be anxious about anything, but in everything, by prayer and petition, with thanksgiving present your request to God. Philippians 4:6

If you know how to give good gifts to your children, how much more will your Father in heaven give good gifts to those who ask Him? Matthew 7:11

Even though I am walking through a valley and the shadow of death is overwhelming, I will not be afraid. Psalm 23:4

Why?

Because God has promised to deliver me. No! Because God has promised to rescue me. No! Because God has promised to defeat my enemy. No!

I will not be afraid because God has promised to be with me in the presence of the enemy. Because God has promised to comfort me in the presence of the enemy. Because God has promised to prepare a table for me in the presence of the enemy.

God has promised to lead me, but I must be willing to follow.

When I pray and I cannot see the hand of God and I cannot hear the voice of God, I will ask myself, "Can I trust the heart of God? Do I trust You, Lord? Do I believe that You do indeed know what I need as I walk through this valley? Do I trust You to lead me when all I can see is the enemy? Can I sit at this table that You have prepared for me and not be anxious for anything?"

If Your goodness and Your love go before me and behind me all the days of my life, like bookends holding everything in its place, then in the midst of chaos and confusion, when I don't know what to do or how to pray, I will be still. I will not be anxious. I will follow You because I know that You are God. I will trust that You have a plan for me, and that it is a good plan. I will trust that Your plan is better than my plan.

Maybe You will deliver me. Maybe You will rescue me. Maybe You will defeat the enemy for me. Maybe You will give me the strength to persevere.

Asking for help does not come easy for most of us. There is a sense of feeling as if we have failed. Why else would we be asking for help? And at a time when we are feeling most vulnerable, the last thing we want is to be judged. Having to explain why we are in the mess we are in contributes to our feeling of failure and defeat. We want to be helped; but we don't want to be judged.

God knows the mess we are in. He knows how we got there. He knows when it all started. He knows what we need before we even begin to pray. He wants to lead us out of the valley. He wants to lead us out of bondage. There is nothing wrong with me bringing my plan to God as long as I am willing to set it aside, in whole or in part, and follow God if He is going in a different direction.

If you are in need, pray believing that God is able to meet your every need.

If you have plenty, give thanks and pray as if all that you have could be lost tomorrow.

Pray believing it is the hand of God that has provided all that you have.

Pray believing that your Father knows what you need before you even ask.

Pray like a child, believing that your very existence is dependent upon the infinite grace of a

loving God.

12

PRAY BECAUSE YOU WANT TO

If you ask me to pray for you, I will. I may ask how I can pray specifically, or I may just pray believing that God knows your need and He knows how best to meet the need. Maybe I will even ask God to use me somehow to meet your need. Maybe I pray because that's what we are supposed to do. We are Christians; we pray for one another.

I'm not proud of this, but there have been times I've prayed as a disinterested third party. "Oh God, someone ask me in faith to pray for them believing that it will make a difference. So here I am, Lord, asking You to help them out." And God meets the need of His child. But it probably had nothing to do with my prayer.

I would rather have one person, who truly wanted to pray for me, praying for me than a bunch of people just going through the motions.

Not long ago, a young girl asked me to pray for her. I said, "I will pray for you. I will pray for you like you were my little girl. But first, I am going to share a story with you. It was a time that God taught this old man a valuable lesson about prayer from a three-year-old."

It happened one night as I was keeping Jax, my grandson, who was almost three years old. It was bedtime, so we brushed our teeth and did all those things we do to get ready for bed. He had a mat beside my bed where he would sleep. As he laid down, I took hold of his little hand and said, "Let's say our prayers." We would pray together first, and then I would always pray for him. Then I would go to the other side of my bed, and I would say my prayers.

Before we began, he said, "Pray for me first."

I said, "You want me to pray for you first?"

He said, "Yes."

He wanted me to pray for him. And he wanted me to pray for him first, so I did.

Without hesitation, I let go of his little hand. I placed my hand upon his forehead and prayed for him. "The Lord bless you and keep you. The Lord makes His face to shine upon you and be gracious unto you. The Lord lifts His countenance toward you and give you peace. Amen."

"Now, let's say our prayers," he said.

I took hold of his little hand again, and we began to pray. "Now I lay me down to sleep. Thank You, Jesus, for loving me. Be with Mommy at work and be with sissy over at Scott's. Be with Mommy when she comes to get me. Bless Mommy, bless sissy, and bless Jax real good. Amen."

As I got up and headed for my side of the bed, he said, "Say your prayers, Dandy."

I said, "Okay," because I didn't want him to know that I didn't feel like praying tonight. I knelt beside my bed and began to reflect upon the challenges of that day and the burdens I had been carrying. What would I say to my God if He were there? Would I say anything at all, or would the tears on my face reveal the pain that I felt? It had been a tough day. It had been a tough week. I had been here before. I was feeling overwhelmed. I was weary. I was oppressed, and I really didn't feel like praying. I wanted someone to pray for me. I had no words.

There are many things I miss about my wife since she died. I miss her smile. I miss her big brown eyes. I miss her touch. I miss holding her. I miss her head laying on my chest at night. I miss waking up next to her. I miss having coffee with her every morning. I miss walking beside her. I miss holding her hand. Sometimes I just miss having someone to talk to.

But I think the thing I miss the most is having someone who loves me to come alongside of me and pray for me.

I desperately needed someone to come alongside me at that moment and pray for me. I was overwhelmed. I was weary. In the silence and the darkness of my empty room, I had reached the point that I was ready to give up.

Like an arrow shot from an archer's bow, the silence was pierced by the unrestrained excitement of a three-year-old. Jax said, "Dandy, I want to pray for you. I want to pray for you, Dandy."

There are moments in our lives that take our breath away. The first time I saw her face, she looked at me with those big brown eyes. She smiled at me; it took my breath away. God was there. He spoke to me. My grandson took my breath away.

He called my name. He called my name and said, "Dandy, I want to pray for you. I want to pray for you, Dandy." Without hesitation, he did not wait for me to answer. He came and stood alongside me as I knelt beside my bed. I bowed my head as tears rolled down my face. I had not said a word, but the Father heard the cry of my heart. He stood by my side and laid his little hand upon the back of my head and began to pray. He prayed for me!

"The Lord bless you . . . and give you peace. Amen."

There may be no such thing as the *perfect prayer*. But that night, in the empty room, beside my bed, I heard my grandson pray a perfect prayer. To be blessed of God and blessed by God, to possess the peace of God, and to be at peace with God. How could I ask for more? When the Spirit intercedes for us in our weakest moments and speaks to God the Father through a child with expressions of love beyond the words of ten thousand tongues, He speaks the perfect prayer.

My grandson called my name and said, "I want to pray for you!" And I'll never forget that.

I looked into the eyes of this young girl. I smiled and said, "I will pray for you now. I will pray for you because I want to pray for you!"

Pray like a three-year-old.

Pray because you want to.

CONCLUSION

The things I learned when my grandson prayed for me:

1.   I learned that God knows my name. He sees my struggles. And in the darkest hour, He calls my name and lifts me up. He is El Roi. Genesis 16:13 He is the God who sees me, when I need a friend to pray for me. He knew what I needed. There was nothing hidden.

2.   I learned that God the Father knows what I need before I even ask. He is Jehovah Shammah. Ezekiel 48:35 He is the Lord who is there. He not only sees me when I am all alone, but He is there with me in

the silence and the solitude. I have learned to talk with God like He is there. I have learned to pray like a child who talks to a friend in the empty chair. He was there.

3.   I learned that God is simple and never complicated. He never intended for life or prayer to be complicated. Love is not complicated. Prayer is not complicated. Life is not complicated through the eyes of a three-year-old. They asked Jesus, "Do you hear what these children are saying?" "Yes," Jesus replied. "Haven't you ever read the Scriptures? For they say, 'You have taught children and infants to give you praise.'" Matthew 21:16 Prayer is not complicated when you pray like a child talking to his Father. His prayer was not complicated.

4.   I learned that God the Father is the answer no matter the question. You will pray, "May the Lord bless you." I will ask, "How can you pray for the Lord to bless me when you don't even know what I need?" God knows! The Son said to ask the Father, "Give us today what we need for this day." Matthew 6:11 He was the answer. He is always the answer. He is always enough.

5.   I learned that prayer is never a little thing with God. The power and effectiveness of a prayer is never measured in the righteousness of the one who prays. The power of prayer is found in God who answers. A little prayer becomes a big thing when it is offered to a big God. It's not the words we say. It's not

the one who prays. It's the God who answers that makes all the difference. Elijah was a man just like us. James 5:17 He prayed that it would not rain. And by the hand of God, the heavens were shut up, and it did not rain on the land for three and a half years. Then he prayed again, and by the hand of God, the heavens were opened, and it rained. There was nothing little or trivial about his prayer.

6.   I learned that God is not moved by the eloquence of our speech, the number of our words, or the grammatical correctness of our prayer. Even when we don't have the words or even know how we ought to pray, He hears the cry of a broken heart. He listens to His children and to the Holy Spirit who intercedes for us with groans that words cannot even express. Romans 8:26 It was simple. His prayer was profoundly simple and simply profound.

7.   I learned that God hears me when I pray. He hears every beat of my heart. He sees every tear I cry. Psalms 56:8 He hears me when I scream. He hears me when I am silent. I have learned to pray like a beggar crying out for mercy. I learned to pray like an only child who has an audience of one with their Father. God heard me through the silence.

8.   I learned that God can speak through His word and God can speak through His Spirit. But sometimes God will speak truth and wisdom out of the mouth of a three-year-old child. God the Father will

hide the deep truth of His word from the wise and learned, from the arrogant and self-righteous, for His good pleasure, and reveal these things to little children. It pleases God to choose the little things of this world to shame the wise. God will choose the weak things to shame the strong. God will use the lowly things and the things that are not to nullify the things that are. God spoke through a child that night.

9.   I have learned that it pleases God the Father when we pray with the persistence of a child. God never grows tired of hearing His children pray. If you pray for rain, pray until it rains! The heavens were opened, and it rained in my room that night.

10.   I have learned to focus on what is really important when I pray. I have learned to pray like I am dying. His prayer was laser focused.

11.   I have learned to pray with the innocence of a child. I have learned to embrace every day to treasure the rose in spite of the thorns. I have learned to live in the moment, to pray in the moment, and to ask for the Father's unconditional blessing. He prayed for the unconditional blessing of God.

12.   I learned that it is better to have one person, who truly wants to pray for me, praying for me than to have a bunch of people just going through the motions. He wanted to pray for me, and that made all the difference.

PRAY LIKE A CHILD

ABOUT THE AUTHOR

Dan Ring is an avid outdoor enthusiast. He is an accomplished long-distance runner, cyclist, and triathlete. He is a city boy who moved to the country and fell in love with a Southern girl. Her name was Debbie. They had three children—Jason, Jennifer, and Adam.

But it was Dan's first grandson, Jaxton that taught this longtime follower of Jesus Christ, Sunday school teacher, and deacon in the Baptist church that life is a lot more fun when you start your day with cartoons and Cocoa Puffs. Life is not that complicated. God is not that complicated. Prayer is not that complicated through the eyes of a three-year-old.

Made in the USA
Coppell, TX
27 August 2020

34429796R00069